PICTURES
TELLING
STORIES
The Art of
Robert Ingpen

Commentary by SARAH MAYOR COX

minedition

Acknowledgements

During the Bologna Children's Book Fair in 2002 an exhibition of non-fiction illustrations displayed some of the pictures we have selected to talk about in this catalogue. At the time a book was proposed because it was suggested that more attention should be given to non-fiction narrative illustration in publishing and picture-book art.

We wish to thank those who have helped with this production. We thank Sarah Mayor Cox for her contribution through studied commentary on the work illustrated. Also thanks to Ermanno Beverari for his high-quality reproduction of the pictures, and Helen Chamberlin for her creative editing skills.

Many people have kindly loaned pictures for use in this catalogue, in particular we thank 'Very Special Kids', Melbourne, and Mr K.T. Hao of Grimm Press, Taiwan. We also want to acknowledge those publishers who have joined Michael Neugebauer Publishing in co-edition of the catalogue.

Angela and Robert Ingpen, Michael Neugebauer, 2004

a minedition book

published by Penguin Young Readers Group

Copyright © 2004 by Robert Ingpen
First American Edition, 2005
Originally published in Hong Kong by Michael Neugebauer Publishing Ltd.
Published simultaneously in Canada.
Manufactured in Hong Kong by Wide World Ltd.
Designed by Michael Neugebauer
Typesetting in Veljovic, designed by Jovica Veljovic.
Color separation by Fotoreproduzioni Grafiche, Verona, Italy.

Library of Congress Cataloging-in-Publication Data available upon request.

ISBN 0-698-40011-9
10 9 8 7 6 5 4 3 2 1
First Impression

For more information please visit our website: www.minedition.com

CONTENTS

Introduction

Stand up and keep your childishness,
Read all the pedant's screeds and strictures,
But don't believe in anything
That can't be told in pictures.
G.K.Chesterton

Everybody loves a story. From the moment humans developed the capacity for speech we have told each other stories. The first were told orally, and soon they were illustrated, perhaps initially with sticks in the dirt, and then more permanently on rocks and cave walls.

Throughout human history stories have been expressed in many different ways and forms. Writers such as Geoffrey Chaucer, William Shakespeare and Gilbert (of Gilbert and Sullivan fame) chose words — written, spoken or sung — to tell their tales. Others, such as Michelangelo and Auguste Rodin, used sculpture. The Bangarra Dance Theatre tells traditional and contemporary Aboriginal stories through dance. Robert Schumann and John Williams use music for their narratives, while tapestries such as the Bayeux Tapestry and the contemporary weavers of the Victorian Tapestry Workshop convey story through the textile arts.

Today, in a world that seems so far from the time of those rock paintings, we still use pictures to tell our stories. Our information age relies more and more on symbols and pictures as our lives get busier and people have less time to read written text. As never before, we are living in a visual age. This book is about how pictures tell stories, how illustrations help to tell the stories of the written texts they accompany and interpret. The Australian illustrator Robert Ingpen has been chosen to explore the role of illustration in story because he has over forty years' experience in the art of illustrating in a vast range of genres.

Since there are dozens of Ingpen's design projects and hundreds of his illustrations and working drawings in existence, it is impossible to present all facets of his work in a book of this size. *Pictures Telling Stories* was never intended to be a biography, nor a comprehensive retrospective of his work. The intention of the book is fourfold. It aims, through captions and essays,

Stonehenge, c. 1560 BC

We do not know what ceremonies Stonehenge played host to in its heyday some 3000 years ago. The effect illustrated of the midsummer sunrise aligning with the Heel Stone and the centre of the monument of great stones must have been awe-inspiring. This reconstruction is based upon current archaeological information. The introduction of a water-filled moat surrounding the site, and creating a 'special island' effect, is speculation.

9

to tell something of the thought processes and intentions behind particular illustrations. It was also written to invite artists to consider a career in illustration as a first option, rather than simply falling back on it, if a career as a fine artist hasn't taken off — or until it does. It is aimed at teachers working with students to help them understand how illustrations can bring to life classic literature, myths and legends, history and people. The over-arching intention, however, is to explore how pictures tell stories — not pictures of the fine art sort, the genre usually associated with prestigious art galleries (although the finest illustrations can of course hold their own against the best fine art) — but pictures of the narrative kind. Pictures which, over the last two centuries, have come to be associated more and more with children's and young adult literature.

N.C. Wyeth, the great American illustrator, is an inspiration for many illustrators, including Ingpen. In a talk published in the *New York Times* on 13 October 1912, Wyeth said:

The artistic powers of an illustrator spring from the same source as do the powers of the painter; but the profound difference lies in the fact that the illustrator submits his inspiration to a definite end; the painter carries his into infinitude. Therefore, the work of the illustrator resolves itself into a craft

It is hoped that reading this book and looking closely at the pictures will offer insights into Ingpen's work and stimulate interest in other illustrators and their creations.

The River,
The Wind in the Willows

In all imaginative literature the description of the environs of the river of Kenneth Grahame's *The Wind in the Willows* is among the most evocative in storytelling and detail.
This overview picture of the scene of events and places in his story attempts to map for the reader a visual guide to the small corner of the dreamy green southern county of England. On one side is the River Bank, crowded with all kinds of 'people' such as Ratty, Mole, Otter, Mr Toad of Toad Hall, and sometimes Badger. On the other side, beyond the watermeadows, is the dark background of the Wildwood. Beyond that again is the Wide World where it is 'all blue and dim'. The animals of the River Bank never venture into the Wide World, except in the reader's imagination.

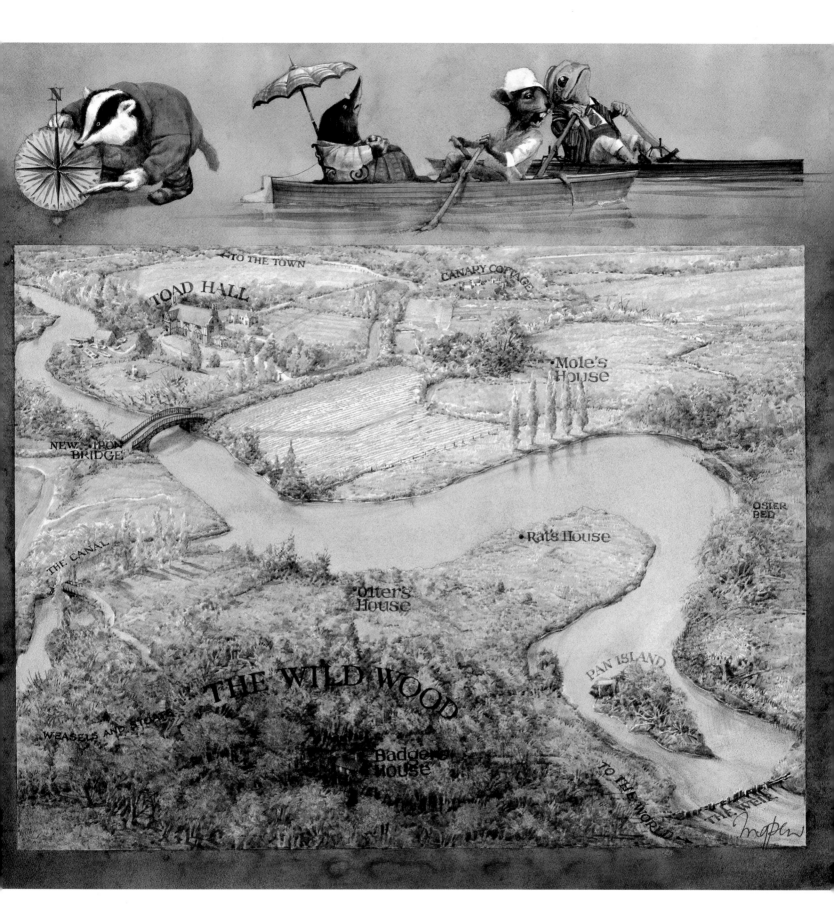

CHAPTER ONE

Pictures Telling Stories in Literature

The Tabard Inn, Southwark, c. 1400 AD

'It happened in that season that one day in Southwark, at The Tabard, as I lay ready to go on pilgrimage and start for Canterbury, most devout at heart, at night there came into that hostelry some nine-and twenty in a company of sundry folk happened then to fall in fellow-ship, and they were pilgrims all that towards Canterbury meant to ride.' [Prologue, *The Canterbury Tales*, Chaucer, 1390]

With Chaucer's word pictures as my guide, I went back to that time to 'witness' that occasion and make illustrations of each of the 'sundry folk', and to make a picture of how the scene might have been that night at the Tabard.

The journey made by the pilgrims from London to Canterbury is part of English history. The pilgrimage and pilgrims described by Geoffrey Chaucer are his own invention. The journey in April would have taken four or five days, and each of his twenty-nine companions told two tales on the way to Canterbury to entertain the travellers. It is generally agreed that in all English literature there is nothing that resembles the Prologue which introduces the pilgrims. It is the concise portrait of an entire nation, high and low, old and young, female and male, lay and clerical, learned and ignorant, rogue and righteous.

The Host of the Tabard Inn

'A very striking man our
Host withal,
And fit to be a marshall
in a hall,
His eyes were bright, his girth
a little wide;
There is no finer burgess in
Cheapside.
Bold in his speech, yet wise
and full of tact,
There is no manly attribute
he lacked ...'

Prologue, *The Canterbury Tales*,
Chaucer

Our Host gave us great welcome; everyone was given a place and supper was begun... A very striking man our Host withal, and fit to be a marshal in a hall. His eyes were bright, his girth a little wide; there is no finer burgess in Cheapside...

The Parson and the Plowman

The Miller

A Holy-minded man of good renown there was, and poor, the parson to a Parson to a town, but he was rich in holy thought and work..
There was a ploughman with him – his brother;
many a load of dung onetime or other he must
have carted ... through the ... morning dew.

The Plowman

The Parson

The Miller was a chap of sixteen stones.
A wrangler and buffoon, he had a
store of tavern stories filthy in the main.
His was a master hand at stealing grain.

The Miller

14

Preliminary Studies for Pilgrims and the Supper Held at
the Tabard, Southwark, April 1390

These studies are only one sheet of many that I need to make as a kind of log to my imaginary journey back in time some six hundred years. From these sketches the final illustrations emerge, and without them the process of creative illustration cannot begin.

An imaginary journey of any distance takes planning and effort, like a real journey over land or sea. The difference is that with an imaginary one you need not leave home. Imagine that every-thing you do in real life happens on a busy highway, and all that we dream about and imagine might be happens on each side of that highway in an endless and seductive forest. The paths to guide you in the forest are those made at previous times by storytellers, inventors, writers and artists. My 'journey' back to the Tabard Inn followed the clear path made by Geoffrey Chaucer so long ago. One reason, perhaps the most important one, for making the journey back to that fabulous place was to keep the path open for readers and dreamers of our present time and for the future.

15

All the time he was jerking out these phrases
he was stumping up and down the tavern
on his crutch, slapping tables with his hand,
giving such a show of excitement—

16

Treasure Island Studies II
Wyeth '91

In *Treasure Island* Stevenson has created the pirate Long John Silver, one of the most enduring characters we have in literature. Most people retain their own mental picture of this famous and feared pirate. Only a few illustrators are lucky enough to be given the challenge of making their picture of him for others to see.

Stevenson introduces him in chapter VIII at the 'Sign of the Spyglass', Bristol, with Jim Hawkins watching ... 'As I waited, a man came out of a side room, and, at a glance, I was sure it must be Long John. His left leg was cut off close to the hip, and under his left shoulder he carried a crutch, which he managed with a wonderful dexterity, hopping about on it like a bird. He was very tall and strong with a face as big as a ham — plain and pale, but intelligent and smiling ...'

Then, throughout the chapter and the story, a fuller word picture is revealed. I felt I needed more information on how he would look as he acted out the events of the story. He was so surprisingly active for a one-legged man with guns and swords and a parrot to carry that I needed some expert help. I talked to a friend who is an orthopaedic surgeon in Geelong, near where I live in Australia. From his experience and advice I made these sketches and studies that became the basis for my final illustrations.

Long John Silver

Robert L. Stevenson carved a clearly marked pathway into the forest of imaginative literature to create *Treasure Island*. Many illustrators have been guided by his storytelling to that fabulous place, and I followed in 1991. I was commissioned to illustrate an edition of the classic adventure story to mark the hundredth year of its publication. A date which more or less coincided with the birth of our grandson, Peter Arch – so I dedicated the new illustrated edition to him.

The illustration appears on the cover of this book, and created a problem regarding Long John Silver's missing left leg. The publisher and designer, Michael Neugebauer, needed the picture of the pirate to be facing the other way to help with the cover design. So, to remain faithful to Stevenson's description, and obedient to the publisher, I made a new illustration so that the left leg, not the right, remained missing.

The Death of Blind Pew

In Chapter 5 of *Treasure Island*, 'The Last of the Blind Man', Blind Pew is deserted by his pirate companions outside the Admiral Benbow Inn, and is observed by Jim Hawkins: 'Him they had deserted whether in sheer panic or out of revenge for his ill words and blows, I know not; but there he remained behind, tapping up and down the road in a frenzy, groping, and calling for his comrades. Finally he took the wrong turn, and ran a few steps past me towards the hamlet, crying: 'Johnny, Black Dog, Dirk,' and other names, 'you won't leave old Pew, mates — not old Pew!'

Just then the noise of horses topping the rise, and four or five riders came in sight in the moonlight, and swept at full gallop down the slope.

At this Pew saw his error, turned with a scream, and ran straight for the ditch into which he rolled. But he was on his feet again in a second, and made another dash, now utterly bewildered, right under the nearest of the coming horses …'

These early chapters of *Treasure Island* remain the most compelling reading in all adventure literature. The greatest illustrated edition is surely the 1911 one with N.C. Wyeth's depiction of Blind Pew. It is often said by experts in reading and literature for children that if a child can read and feel the drama of the happenings at the Benbow Inn as imagined by Robert L. Stevenson, then they will be readers forever.

Study for Blind Pew
Ingpen 91

Shakespeare

Recently I collaborated with British writer Michael Rosen to make a book on the work and world of William Shakespeare for teenagers who could expect to have to read one of his plays at school. Walker Books hoped that by publishing this book, children would be better introduced to Shakespeare.

The kind of stories Shakespeare invites you to make pictures for are very different from those of Stevenson. His language is similar, but his purpose and impact has a special power. He didn't really write books, he wrote scripts — scenes and speeches for people to say aloud and act out in front of other people in theatres and playhouses. Shakespeare knew, as an actor, just how powerful this can be.

He wrote an incredible set of stories, full of action, poetry, tension, love, death, fun, music, dance, war, rebellion, conspiracy and betrayal. Sometimes they are about politics, at other times about how people get on together as man and woman, parent and child, friend and friend.

SHAKESPEARE AT WORK

PEOPLE ARGUE ABOUT EXACTLY HOW MANY PLAYS SHAKESPEARE WROTE. BECAUSE WE KNOW THAT HE SHARED THE WRITING OF SEVERAL OF THEM. THAT'S WHY.

OF THESE THINGS.

This doesn't tell us.

56

Working Plans for Shakespeare Page Spreads

To begin my part in this production I made many 'flat plans' which laid out the pages and sequence of how we might arrange the book. Working with the publishing team and with the writer, these were refined and tailored to tell much about Shakespeare and yet leave out, or leave to the reader's imagination, so much that could never be put into a 96-page book. Some of the early plans are reproduced here.

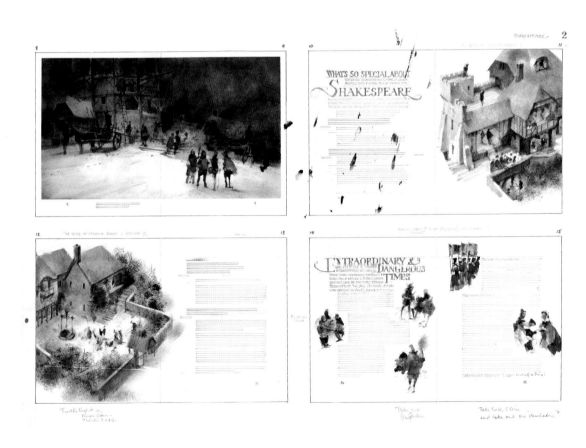

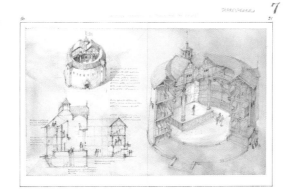

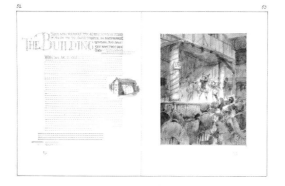

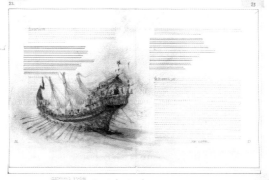

following pages

A Plot!

The final book begins by illustrating an extraordinary event that reveals much about Shakespeare's life and times …

'It's the middle of the night on the edge of London, a few days after Christmas Day 1598. The River Thames is frozen over, snow is falling. The roofs of the timbered houses and the nearby fields are white with it. Four buildings stand higher than the nearby houses. One is a theatre, simply called the Theatre. Tonight, sixteen men are pulling down the Theatre. Two of them are brothers. They run a company of actors who put on plays, and with them are a builder and his workmen. As the men hurry about their work, it's clear that what's going on is secret and must be done as quickly as possible.

Through the night the workmen load timbers onto wagons. Two strangers arrive and start quizzing them. The workmen lie and say they are taking down only parts of the building that are decaying. Really, they are dismantling the whole theatre and taking it somewhere else. It's a risky business because if it can be proved that they are stealing, they will all be hanged and their severed heads put on show. But before long the men, who include William Shakespeare, are taking the timbers across London Bridge to Southwark, where the theatre will be rebuilt and become known as one the world's most famous theatres: the Globe.

Southwark, London, 1600 AD

In Shakespeare's plays we meet the people of London. We meet the residents and the visitors from other places he could never travel to. He lived here beside the Thames, close to London Bridge (top left) and in the shadow of the Globe. To make this illustration I spent time in Southwark again, but this time I actually walked the streets in search of Shakespeare and his time four hundred years ago.

I drew upon what is left of those extraordinary and dangerous times and what has been re-created to remember Elizabethan London. The new Globe Theatre on the site very near this recreated streetscape was a great source of reference for my journey to make the picture. But most influential was the writing of Shakespeare. His creative vision, focus on detail and his sense of drama and fun all guided me to show others what his world might have looked like.

Cleopatra's Barge

We do not know enough about Shakespeare's life to be sure
where he got his plots and characters for his plays. We know
that sometimes he changed the great words he found in old
books and put them into the mouths of his characters, as he did
with the description of Cleopatra floating down the river in a
golden barge. He adapted a rather matter-of-fact report by the
Roman writer Plutarch into his own words, written in 1606:

'The barge she sat in, like a burnished throne
Burned on the water. The poop was beaten gold;
Purple the sails, and so perfumed that
The winds were love-sick with them. The oars were silver,
Which to the tune of flutes kept stroke, and made
The water which they beat to follow faster,
As amorous of their strokes!'

Antony and Cleopatra, act 2, scene 2, lines 198–204

Robinson Crusoe

In 1719 Daniel Defoe published *The Life and Strange Surprising Adventures of Robinson Crusoe*. Possibly based on a few facts, he proposed that Robinson Crusoe lived mostly alone on an island off the north-east coast of South America for twenty-eight years. As sole survivor of a shipwreck, and with great ingenuity, he managed to survive and even to protect himself against cannibals and marooned seafarers. He returned finally to have Defoe tell an enduring story that is still published with its old words and new pictures today.

The Empire of Lilliput

In 1726 Jonathan Swift published in Dublin *The Travels into Several Remote Nations of the World*, by Lemuel Gulliver. We still read and admire the ingenuity and social commentary of this great work of literature, which has been the basis for much modern 'fantasy' storytelling. The illustration here depicts the ritual Swift proposes for political pre-selection and appointment. When a ministerial office falls vacant in the Empire of Lilliput, the candidates are obliged to entertain the emperor and his court by dancing and jumping on a tightrope set at a dangerous distance above the ground. Those who jump highest and dance most nimbly receive the most important appointments, but many applicants meet with fatal accidents during their exertions. This ritual is repeated at regular intervals during their terms of office, to determine whether they are still fit to serve.

Lilliput
Diſcoverd
A.D. 1699

Mildendo

31

Pictures Telling Stories in Literature

Previous pages

The Sledge across the Prairie

In 1872 Jules Verne published *Around The World in Eighty Days*. Although we live in an age when round-the-world travel is possible in hours rather than weeks, Jules Verne's tale of a race against the clock has never lost its power to thrill or to capture the imagination of illustrators.

Phileas Fogg leaves the comfort of the Reform Club in London with his companion Passepartout to ride through India on an elephant, sail through cyclones, cross oceans in borrowed ships, and to 'sail' across the snow-covered plains of America's Wild West.

It may seem strange to include characters and situations from works of fiction in a book about non-fiction illustration, but Ingpen doesn't think of these stories in terms of the conventional definition of fiction as something 'made up'. He does not refute that writers invent the characters and stories, but he terms them 'literary' or 'narrative' non-fiction because, as classics, they have made their way into our cultural heritage. They are so well known that they have become reference points for life, in much the same way as we use non-fiction as a reference point for works of fiction. In everyday life we sometimes refer to characters from the great classics of literature as if they were real people. When people describe a position as being a job for a 'Man Friday', or term someone who has a changing personality as a bit of a 'Jekyll and Hyde', or talk about wanting to 'do a Clancy', they are calling up what these characters and stories have come to represent. Often this is done without stopping to think about the origins of the characters, and people who have not actually read the original stories still use these terms and have a vague understanding of their meaning.

In his book, *Illustrating Children's Books: History, Technique, Production (Watson-Guptill, New York, 1963)*, Henry Pitz points out that 'every year some of them [adult classics] are reprinted and re-illustrated for a new audience' and so publishers will be on the lookout for illustrators to bring these stories to a new generation of readers. Ingpen made a similar claim when talking about his illustrations for *Treasure Island*, which will be discussed in more detail later in this chapter: 'The words are set and they won't be changed, but [*Treasure Island*] is still one of the great adventure stories, so every generation or so it will be illustrated.'

Nicolas Flamel and the Philosopher's Stone

Legend has it that in the 14th century French alchemist Nicolas Flamel obtained the ancient magical text that revealed the secret of how to transform mercury into gold — the Philosopher's Stone.

In modern literature Flamel lives on, as readers of '*Harry Potter and the Philosopher's Stone*' by J. K. Rowling well know. It was Flamel's Stone that the evil wizard Voldemort tried but failed to steal, thanks to Harry Potter's heroic intervention.

Making pictures to tell stories in literature allows an illustrator to demonstrate his or her ability to handle two important requirements of non-fiction illustration, both of which are underlying themes in Ingpen's work — the importance of space and the need to be useful.

Space is what an illustrator builds into pictures so that just enough detail about the setting and casting of a story is included, while leaving out enough detail for readers to use their imaginations and make the story their own. Ingpen's illustrations of Chaucer's and Shakespeare's works are good examples of this. Ingpen chose to illustrate most of the twenty-nine characters Geoffrey Chaucer described in the prologue to *The Canterbury Tales*, as they assembled at the Tabard Inn in 1390 before setting out on their pilgrimage to the shrine of Thomas-a-Becket.
He also illustrated the Host of the inn (p. 13) and, in his final illustration for this section of *Once upon a Place*, an imaginary but very probable meal which the Host might have served before all the pilgrims set off.

In commenting on the careful research he needed to do to make pictures of Chaucer's colourful characters, Ingpen noted:

'People have given all sorts of reasons for Chaucer not taking his pilgrims all the way to Canterbury, or bringing them back. I don't think it was an accident, or that he tired of the story. I think Chaucer knew his readers could do that for themselves with the help of space left for their imagination.'

With this help from Chaucer in mind, he has also left lots of space for the reader. Although he has used Chaucer's words to determine the appearance of the Host — 'His eyes were bright, his girth a little wide' —, the illustration also shows that the Host has lost a tooth, possibly in a fight. By including this detail Ingpen invites the reader to look further into the story. Although he is careful to illustrate accurately, accuracy does not mean taking the text too literally. Chaucer does not mention that the Host has lost a tooth but, knowing what we do about dental hygiene, nutrition and law and order in the Middle Ages, it is probable.

What Ingpen was trying to do by illustrating the prologue rather than the whole of *The Canterbury Tales* was to take the reader back to the Tabard Inn as it would have been when the pilgrims set out for Canterbury, and to draw the pilgrims as Chaucer described them so that, with a better understanding of the time frame and characters, readers could discover the story for themselves.

The Yeoman

In Chaucer's words: 'There was a Yeoman ... His head was like a nut, his face was brown. He knew the whole of wood-craft up and down. A saucy brace was on his arm to ward it from the bow-string, and a shield and sword hung at one side ...'

There was a Yeoman... ...his head was like a nut, his face was brown. He knew the whole of woodcraft up and down. A saucy brace was on his arm to ward it from the bow-string, and a shield and sword hung at one side, and at the other tipped a jaunty ... he was a proper forester.

36

Whenever Ingpen illustrates literary non-fiction, he follows a 'strict set of illustration processes', so that the illustrations support the text and help the reader. This is perhaps one of his greatest skills, and no doubt one of the reasons he has been commissioned to illustrate so many classics and books chronicling famous people and events.

Ingpen first committed himself to following these processes when he specialised in a subject called 'Art of the Book' while studying for a diploma in art and design at the Royal Melbourne Institute of Technology from 1955-8. Although he does see book illustration as an art form, he believes that illustrations need to serve the words or the ideas, rather than existing as art forms in their own right. This is especially true of illustrations for classic literature. Ingpen believes it is important not only to support the text, but also to take it further. However, he is also acutely aware of the fine line an illustrator walks between useful interpretation — interpreting classic stories so they are made accessible to a new generation — and obtrusive interpretation that is too concerned with raising the illustrator's profile.

In explaining why two of his best known books, *The Idle Bear* (1986) and *The Dreamkeeper* (1994), would not be included in *Pictures Telling Stories*, Ingpen said that he had wanted to include only 'works of preservation'. He sees it as an illustrator's responsibility to preserve classics in literature, in preference to making pictures for his own stories or for texts that are in 'fashion' at the moment.

Ingpen has a metaphor with which he likes to explain what he means by preservation — or even conservation — of literature and storytelling. He sometimes calls it 'the forest and the highway', or 'the forest of the imagination'. Asking him the familiar question, 'Where do stories come from?' will also elicit a reference to this metaphor. It is explained in his caption for his 'Preliminary studies for pilgrims and the supper held at the Tabard, Southwark, April 1390 (p.14), where he describes his preservation work as 'clearing the old tracks and paths to and from the highway through the deep forest of the imagination'. These tracks, he says, were made long ago by writers such as Chaucer, or more recently, Australia's Patricia Wrightson. When he illustrates his own stories, on the other hand, he is cutting new paths of his own.

Preservation is a theme running through much of Ingpen's work, and the chronology on pp. 107–9 reveals how much of his work is concerned with conservation — of buildings, history and the environment as well as of stories. He thinks it is important not only to keep classic and enduring literature alive by ensuring that it is illustrated in each generation, but also to pay homage to great artists who have gone before by making visual reference to their style or particular works. Ingpen has been influenced greatly by two artists: the American illustrator N.C.Wyeth (1882-1945);

Alice's Dream of Wonderland

The principal wonderland of the British Isles, as described by a lecturer in mathematics, Lewis Carroll, in 1865, is a subterranean community lying beneath the Oxfordshire countryside. It is entered through a girl-size rabbit hole (top left) and runs into literature's most fabulous dream sequence. Over the years *Alice's Adventures in Wonderland* has been published with many kinds and styles of illustration. This attempt to contain the dream sequence and its crazy events within the one picture is to be seen as a game of visually following the events leading one from another.

and Pieter Bruegel the Elder (1525-69), the sixteenth-century master of 'genre pictures'. He describes these artists as 'quiet observers', from whom he has learnt much about the role composition, perspective, light and space play in getting the heart of a story or an idea into the minds of readers.

Understanding that Ingpen is deliberately trying to be a quiet observer helps the reader or viewer understand his pictures in which, in his own words, 'nothing much is happening '. These 'quiet' illustrations are not merely decorative — they are just different from interpretive illustrations. Not only do they reveal Ingpen's confidence in his own drawing style but, more importantly, his confidence in us as capable and responsive readers. He sees his readers as the kind who, given enough accurate details of place and humanity and enough imaginative space, will be able to work things out for ourselves. Here the influence of Bruegel is most obvious.

One of the best examples of Ingpen as a quiet observer — and by no coincidence one of his favourite illustrations from his book on Shakespeare — is the 'Stratford Market Day' picture (pp. 2–3). Ingpen described it as follows:

'It's hot and Shakespeare's there. You know he's there. He's a kid — he's about the age of those people who've got to get excited about this [Shakespeare book] and he's watching these players who are just there in a heat haze, a shimmering sort of mirage in this smelly market place in 1560.'

His illustration of 'Southwark, London, 1600 AD' (pp. 26–7) can be viewed as a companion to 'Stratford Market Day'. He has gone to great lengths to ensure that the details of this illustration are accurate. He uses this detail as a background against which he has illustrated a bustling scene in which nothing in particular is happening, but everything is happening too. The reader can enter that busy scene and wander around, taking in the sights, sounds and smells which inspired Ingpen in the first place.

Leaving enough imaginative space is crucial in varying the speed at which a story unfolds and in enhancing and echoing the written text. Ingpen's double-page spread to accompany 'A Plot', which opens the Shakespeare book, does just that. In explaining the origins of the Globe Theatre, Michael Rosen's text builds a tension which is heightened as the reader turns the page to find the scene waiting to be explored (pp. 24–5). The night has fallen and the wooden wheels on the cart indicate the depth of snow. We don't exactly know how far into the night it is, but we can see there is a lot more work to be done before morning. And knowing that the two strangers questioning the three 'builders' in the bottom right of the picture have the potential to change the course of history, our eyes are drawn up to the left of the picture where we anxiously glance over the partly deconstructed theatre and wonder just what would have happened if the strangers had not believed the actors' 'well-crafted' story.

Thankfully, Shakespeare did get away with the move and went on to write some of the funniest, most tragic and most thought-provoking plays ever written in English. One of the things Ingpen wanted his illustrations for Shakespeare to do was to find ways of exemplifying Shakespeare's genius. In his illustration of Cleopatra's barge (pp. 28–9), he is trying to show not only the splendour and majesty of her vessel (which would have seemed beyond exotic to the ordinary English folk attending his plays), but also the splendour of Shakespeare's words. He does this by a visual reference to the English artist J.M. Turner , who Ingpen lists as another influential artist in his life.

Turner's influence in this work can be seen in Ingpen's use of colour, subject and composition, reminiscent of many of Turner's landscape paintings of sunsets and sunrises over water. Ingpen has the barge emerging from a magical haze, infused with brilliant sunshine. He has called on a technique which he felt would best represent mystery and grandeur, so that the reader would have the 'space' needed to take in Shakespeare's poetic capturing of the the exotic.

There is another example of Ingpen's use of imaginative space in the endpapers of *Pictures Telling Stories*. They are of *A Midsummer Night's Dream* and were chosen because so many people say that they love Ingpen's pencil and wash work best. He is baffled but pleasantly surprised by this, and in his typically understated and facetious way, describes this technique as 'the sloshy, washy stuff I do in pencil and then just wash over. [It] leaves mystery and space, and it's that wash that leaves room for other people to get into.' The background, gossamer-like wash of the endpapers captures the enchanted whimsy of this play and the yellowish ribbon of wash which sweeps over the top indicates the enchantments weaving themselves in and out of the characters' relationships in the play.

The accuracy in Ingpen's work springs from hours of research and preparatory intellectual work. For Long John Silver in *Treasure Island* (pp. 16–17) he consulted an orthopaedic surgeon to find out how an amputee like Long John Silver could be so active. This work was necessary because Ingpen was confronting an illustrative dilemma — to make 'pictures that are convincing without destroying the pictures that are richly established in the mind of everybody '.

Pitz (in *Illustrating Children's Books: History, Technique, Production, Watson-Guptill, New York, 1963*) stresses that an 'illustrator is forced to know his subject and have

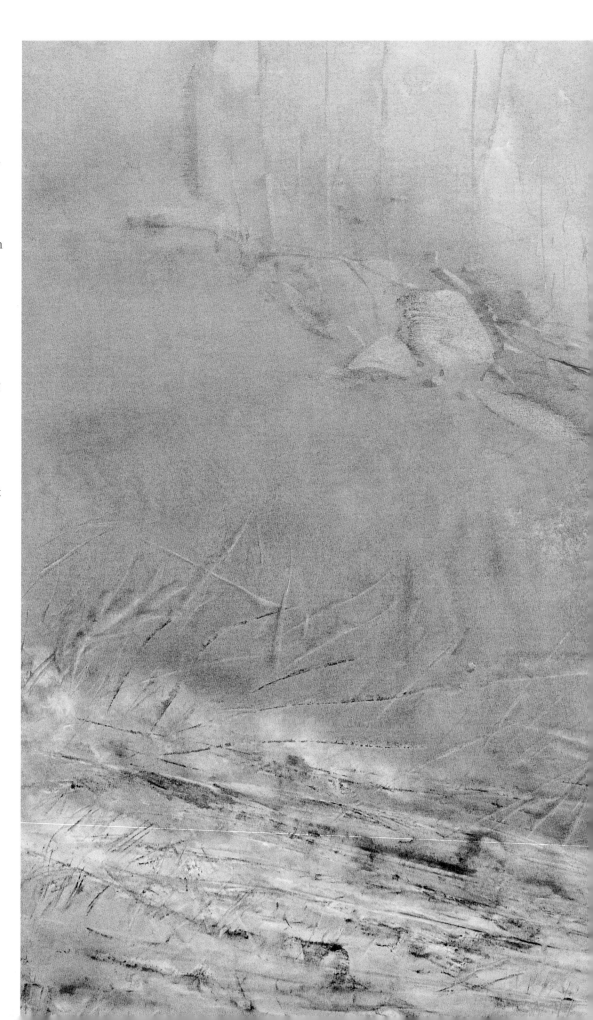

Clancy of the Overflow

In 1889 A. 'Banjo' Paterson wrote the ballad 'Clancy of the Overflow' to express the division he felt in his own life between living in the city of Sydney, Australia, and the dream of being in the country — the outback of Australia. It was published in the *Bulletin,* in December 1889, and achieved immediate and lasting popularity, as Paterson seemed to show the real Australia.

'And I somehow rather fancy that I'd like to change with Clancy,
Like to take a turn at droving where the seasons come and go,
While he faced the round eternal of the cashbook and the journal
But I doubt he'd suit the office, Clancy of the Overflow.'

This legendary bushman of Banjo Paterson's verse may never have existed. But does it matter? He is, to most Australians, a very real, even larger-than-life figure, a free and independent spirit galloping through the wide open spaces of the 'outback' and of our imagination — vigorous, hearty and carefree. And that is how I tried to picture him telling his story.

reasons for everything he does.' He also argues that illustrators must couple this visual accuracy with 'bounce and elasticity in [their] work'. If you compare Ingpen's illustrations of *Treasure Island* with N.C. Wyeth's (1911), you will find that Ingpen's 'bounce and elasticity' are hard at work to bring characters like Long John Silver and Blind Pew to life for a new generation.

Since Wyeth's edition was published we have had another eighty years of story-telling on film and in books. As a result many illustrators today use quite filmic angles of vision, because their readers understand what these angles mean. The different vantage points they provide allow the illustrator to draw attention to a particular feature of a character or situation, such as Ingpen has done with 'The Death of Blind Pew' (pp. 18–19). He has changed the angle at which we view Blind Pew between the study and the final illustration — so accentuating Blind Pew's precarious situation.

Ingpen insists that it is 'no use saying other people have their own impressions' and walking away from the challenge of illustrating such well-known characters. The key to illustrating classics, after leaving space and being accurate, is in finding the essence of the scene or character and representing that visually. To that end Ingpen has drawn on the vulnerability he found in Long John Silver to capture Robinson Crusoe (p. 30). He explains, 'He's very proud of himself, [the portrait] sort of echoes Long John Silver … Robinson Crusoe is vulnerable, although he's trying not to be.' Ingpen uses a limited range of colours to illustrate the relationship between Crusoe and his habitat and includes an umbrella fashioned from materials on the island to remind us that Crusoe is locked into that landscape. Although he tries to look confident, the background is very flat, so that he almost looks stuck on, in a vulnerable, super-imposed way, instead of merging with it.

More than 100 illustrators have illustrated versions of *Alice's Adventures in Wonderland*. Ingpen has not illustrated a complete edition, but his story map of 'Alice's Dream' (pp. 38–9) provides a complete visual scaffold for the reader. Story-mapping is a technique that many teachers use to give their students an overview of a story. Younger readers can often be as disorientated as Alice herself in the crazy world of the book. By laying out the major plot points of the story, starting with Alice in reality (he has used watercolour to represent the 'real' bits and pencil and wash for the dream sequence), Ingpen is able to help the reader understand things that may not have been clear from the written text. This illustration is not unlike a game board where the game is laid out before you and you have to make the fun.

It is fitting that Clancy of the Overflow should be the last literary character in this chapter. For non-Australians he may simply be a well-known figure of classic colonial literature. However, in the same way that King Arthur stirs up feelings of longing for another way of doing things, and Beowulf represents man's ability to tackle the impossible, so for many Australians Clancy represents national characteristics we like to revere publicly — bucking the system and following one's dreams. Australia may well be one of the most urbanised and multicultural countries in the world, but there is still a romantic notion of escaping the city and fleeing to the 'bush'. Robert has represented Clancy's skillful horsemanship and set his confident and daring stance against the harsh colours of the Australian bush. In so doing he has captured Clancy's 'vigorous, hearty and carefree' nature and brought it alive for a new generation of readers.

Juliet's Soliloquy

In real life, people don't often make speeches out loud when they're on their own, but in Shakespeare's plays we find ourselves listening to these speeches and what they tell us about the workings of the mind. Here's Juliet in the play *Romeo and Juliet* talking to herself and us:
Come night, come Romeo; come, thou day in night,
For thou wilt lie upon the wings of night
Whiter than new snow on a raven's back.
Come, gentle night:
come, loving, black-browed night.
Romeo and Juliet, act 3, scene 2, lines 17–20

In the background is a detail of a street wall decoration not far from Juliet's imaginary home in old Verona, Italy.

45

CHAPTER TWO # Folk Tales and Myths at Work

The Drover's Boy

Australian folklorist Ted Egan
wrote 'The Drover's Boy' as a
song of fiction but it is based
on indisputable historical
fact. Not so long ago, when
'white men' took reprisals
against a group of Aboriginal
people they often abducted
the women. These women
became virtual slaves.
Dressed as boys, they worked
without pay to move cattle all
over Australia. Yet in some
cases, as the song suggests,
genuine love between the
drover's 'boys' and their white
bosses developed out of
mutual dependence.

**Momotaro —
the Peach-Boy**

A classic folk tale of Japan
containing instruction in the
virtues of one's family duty
and knowing one's status
in society as a Samurai.
Among Momotaro's constant
companions is a dog. I chose
to use our family dog, Ben, as
the model in this illustration.

Beowulf

The story of the Anglo-Saxon
hero Beowulf began some time
between the ninth and twelfth
centuries as a poem. He lives
still in our imagination as the
slayer of Grendel the Fiend.

The Pedlar of Swaffham

In the village of Swaffham,
Norfolk, there lived a
pedlar who was plagued by
a certain dream. If he stood
on London Bridge he would
hear joyful news. That
story began 400 years ago
and continues to be told in
a wide range of versions.

Hamelin Town, Germany, c. 11th Century AD

Long ago in ancient Germany, at a time just on the brink of modern civilisation, something terrible happened in Hamelin Town. Somehow we will never know, during those days of crusades, continental wars and the horror of the Black Plague, the children of Hamelin Town were lost forever.

With no real explanation of what happened, and no modern grief counselling to call upon, people eventually turned to storytelling to ease the pain and help come to terms with something they couldn't understand.

They invented a story about a stranger known as the 'Pied Piper', who promised the elders of Hamelin that he would use his magical pipe-playing to rid the town of a plague of rats.

He was as good as his word, but when he asked for his payment the town elders refused. The next day the streets of Hamelin were silent. The children were all gone, except for one crippled boy, who told his story ...

The story of the Pied Piper has become a folktale. The modern town of Hamelin in Westphalia is much changed since those times in the thirteenth century but the Rattenfangerhaus (or Rat-catcher's House) can still be seen.

Are Religions Fairy Stories?

Religious people would say to people who think that religions are just fairy stories; 'Well then, how would you try to answer the *big* and *deep* questions? What have you got to say about the beginning of everything, and the importance of human life, and why we should be good, and why there is evil? Can you explain these things without some kind of religious belief?'

To illustrate this wisdom, I made my adapted version of one of the biblical stories of the great flood and Noah. The story is 'The Raven and the Dove', and the original illustration is from Folio 8, *Holkham Bible Picture Book*, 14th Century.

Noah's Ark in the Deluge

Here is a new story tailoring the old story of Noah's Ark to our modern environmental and conservation crisis.

Imagine that in the whole world there is still one treasure to be found. That is Noah's log of his journey with all the animals on the Ark.

We all know the 'fairy story' of Noah's Ark; the vessel he built so long ago to save his family and most of the world's animals from the great flood that was to drown the world. But we have never found a trace of the Ark, or any ancient clay tablet that might suggest the story is true. We have never, so far, looked for Noah's log of the voyage. We do not know that we have to look into our imagination to recover what he might have written.

If we looked for a real document that recorded the names and needs of all the creatures that came aboard and were saved, and those that did not and were lost, we would never find it. But we can, and must, pretend what it would be like, and learn so that if today we need to save our world, we can imagine and believe in what must be done.

The Tower of Babel Today

The story of the Tower of Babel appears in the Bible (Genesis 11:1-9). After the flood, Noah's descendants came to the land of Shinar, where they learned to build huge brick monuments. There, so the story goes, they created a lasting memorial — a tower that reached all the way to heaven. But God saw the building of the tower as an act of arrogance, and disrupted their work with a trick. He mixed up their languages, so confusing them that they could not understand and communicate with each other.

Throughout history, we have been fascinated by this story and what it means. Is it a story of the arrogance of humanity? Is it about the problems we can expect in our lives from archaeological and human technical development? Or is it about language, human communication and the information revolution?

I have drawn the present stage of growth of the Tower of Babel. In 500 years it has grown greatly from the most famous picture of it painted by illustrator Pieter Breugel. His version is almost hidden at centre left of the massive construction.

52

Plans for the Banquet Hall on Tara Hill

Many years ago I remember being fascinated by a fragment of fact. I had read that, 'on the northern slope of Tara Hill (County Meath) two parallel banks mark the site of Teach Miodchuarta — the Banquet Hall. Though desolate today, this place was once the home of heroes. It is said that here the Feis Teamharch — the Banquet of Heroes — was held.' I even found seating plans for banquet guests in old Celtic manuscripts.

I drew these imaginary plans for the Banquet Hall in order to establish a 'place' for a great banquet of heroes of myth, legend and folklore to be enacted.

The Banquet of Heroes, Tara Hill

For the purpose of 'giving voice' to heroes who continue to inspire our 'inner lives' in story, if not in reality, I invented my own banquet.

At the conclusion of my book *Once upon a Place* I wrote:

'The Banquet of Heroes at Tara was different from all others and can only be imagined. It was Lugh of the Long Arm, a figure of Irish legend, who ordered the special feast to honour the heroes and heroines of the myths, folktales and stories of all ages. Invitations were sent and a hundred heroes came across oceans, over continents and from the Cosmos. The Banquet Hall was filled (as you can see) with people who crossed boundaries of culture, religion, time and reality. They represented all of our imagination, its dreams, hopes and potential.

Each guest was required to make a speech during the week of banqueting, and in the speech they were to tell us mortals why we should remember them ...'

Here is a list of some of the guests who attended the imaginary Banquet of Heroes on Tara Hill:

Arthur of Camelot	Sir Thomas More
St Ursula	Mary
Beowulf (see p. 46)	Catherine of Alexandria
Gilgamesh	St Francis of Assisi
St George	Pocahantas
	Martin Luther
	Odin
	Athene
	Judith

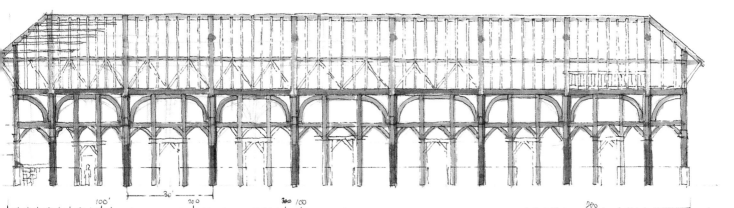

Sigurd of the Volsungs
Hildegard von Bingen
Quetzalcoatl
Odysseus
Vainnamoinen
Aphrodite
Gandhi
Cucchulain
Galileo Galilei

Medea
Catherine of Siena
Rahab of Jericho
Esther
Demeter
Boadicea
El Cid
Roland
Moses

John Lennon
Robin Hood
Mary Bryant
Paul Bunyan
Heracles
Merlin
Bilqis
Scheherazade
Clancy

Atalanta
Maui
St Joan
Leonardo da Vinci
Perseus

ATLANTIS CITY

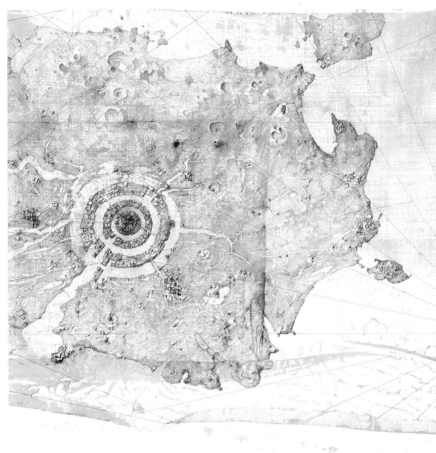

The Destruction of Atlantis

Atlantis was first mentioned by Plato, but Greek myths and legends touched upon this lost place. Without a map as a guide, it seemed the place may continue to be lost, even to our imagination. To have a map would at least show us what it looked like, even if we couldn't go there.

When the great Greek gods divided up the universe, the lord of the oceans, Poseidon, established the beautiful state and city of Atlantis for himself. Built around concentric circles of water and land, it became the world centre of culture and science. But when the people of Atlantis stopped obeying Poseidon's laws, the city was swallowed up by the ocean forever (see pp. 58–9).

59

The Poppykettle Adventure

In the early 1970s I was working in Peru for the United Nations (FAO/UNDP). Our team was recruited to study the influence of an El Nino episode on the massive commercial anchovy fishery of Peru. Part of my work in helping improve communication within the fishing industry was to search for old folk stories that had been handed down since the days of the Inca civilisation that related to fishing practice. I found a story that seemed to be told by pelicans that concerned the sea-god El Nino, and this was particularly useful when modified to promote new fishing science and conservation ideas to local fishing communities. Later, the same tale, further adapted, became the basis for the 'Poppykettle Stories'.

Poppykettle is the name of a special Peruvian clay teapot. When it was converted to a floating vessel, a crew of Hairy Peruvian dolls sailed away in it from their homeland, which was under attack from Shining Spaniards, to find a new home. They were 'Boat People'. The Poppykettle Stories were designed as new folktales to help reveal the plight and saga of Boat People, whoever they may be. A number of versions of the story have been written, illustrated and published over the years between 1980 and 2000, and more may yet appear. There is *The Voyage of the Poppykettle,* 1980, *The Unchosen Land,* 1981, and *The Poppykettle Papers,* 1999.

My home town of Geelong was the landing place of the Peruvian expedition some 400 years ago. To mark this the community did two things. They built a fountain on the Geelong waterfront which was popular for many years with children and families, until it was replaced with a car park. Also they created the idea that primary school children should celebrate imagination with a holiday every early November, and they called it 'Poppykettle Day'. This has been an annual event on the education calendar in the Geelong district for over twenty years.

Over this time I have been able to observe the progress of this folktale knowing that it is composed of a mix of facts, unexplained events — possible facts and pure fiction that drives the excitement in adventure stories.

As in all enduring stories there remains much to be discovered by new readers, and much space for imaginative people to make modifications to the story to suit the occasion and the audience. The things that remain constant in the re-telling of the stories are often surprising. The Silver Fish, for example, had only a small part in the early stories, but now, as if by popular request, it has caught people's imagination.

60

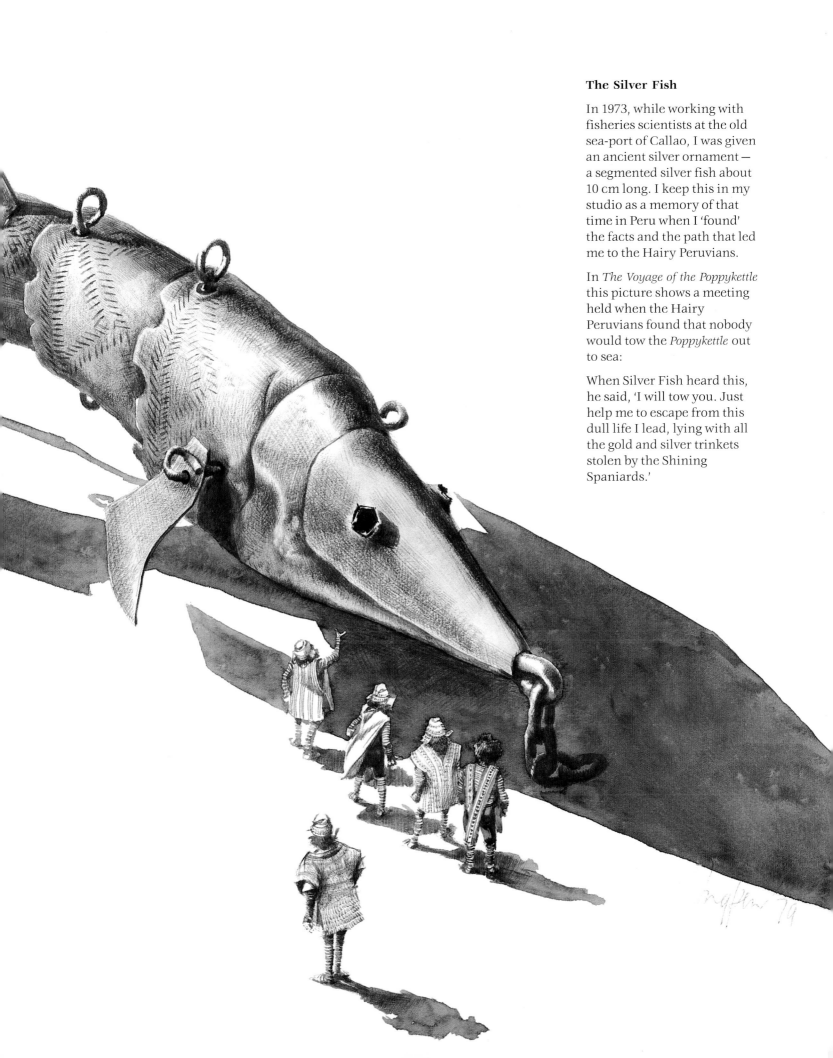

The Silver Fish

In 1973, while working with fisheries scientists at the old sea-port of Callao, I was given an ancient silver ornament — a segmented silver fish about 10 cm long. I keep this in my studio as a memory of that time in Peru when I 'found' the facts and the path that led me to the Hairy Peruvians.

In *The Voyage of the Poppykettle* this picture shows a meeting held when the Hairy Peruvians found that nobody would tow the *Poppykettle* out to sea:

When Silver Fish heard this, he said, 'I will tow you. Just help me to escape from this dull life I lead, lying with all the gold and silver trinkets stolen by the Shining Spaniards.'

ARNICA — NAVIGATOR

ASTUTE — NEGOTIATOR

Preliminary Poppykettle Studies

Well before I began writing the words for the Poppykettle tales, I made these drawings of the characters and events I had in mind. I made notes that I might need for the imagined clay vessel that was to become the *Poppykettle*, and sketched both the outside and inside of the pot as a kind of kettlewright's plans. Each of the Hairy Peruvian crew begin to appear in drawings and be characterised before being written down. They are Don Avante — the leader, Arnica — the futureteller, Astute — the navigator and translator, Arnago — the cook and nurse, Arrant and Andante — crewmen, and Aloof — the lookout. Each is endowed with special skills that are available only to partly human dolls like Hairy Peruvians.

62

EL NINO

DON AVANTE - LEADER

ARRANT - CREWMAN

ARNAGO - COOK

ANDANTE - CREWMAN

ALOOF - LOOKOUT

The Friendly Dolphin

Towards the end of *The Voyage of the Poppykettle* the crew of surviving Hairy Peruvians are rescued after a great storm has broken their clay pot — the *Poppykettle* (see p. 62).

A curious and friendly dolphin comes to save them: 'He could not help them during the storm, but when he saw them sinking he swam up and said, 'I'll lift you out of the water with my head. You'd better work out some way of holding on, and then I'll carry you along with me.'

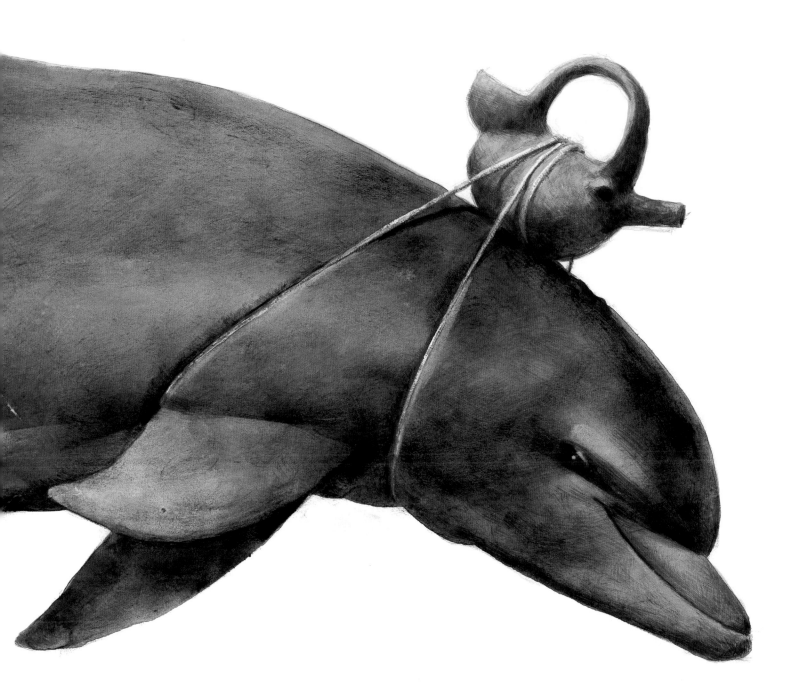

Folk Tales and Myths at Work

'Myths are more than just stories: every myth is a shaft of human truth. One person's myth is another's religious belief; one person's truth another's fiction.'

Neil Philip (1995)

The invention of the printing press had two major effects on stories. Printing made written versions of stories more accessible, due to the number produced and the reduced cost, and it brought into being the idea of one version of a story becoming more prominent than others. Until then it was a given that each storyteller told a tale in his or her own unique style, and that even the same story was never fixed. Depending on the time of the year it was told, in what company, and for what reason, different parts of the story were accentuated or left out altogether. Stories were much more fluid then than they are today.

Most people first come across traditional literatures during their childhood, since many of these stories, especially folk tales, fairy tales and wonder tales, have been recast for children. Often the versions they have been read, in the west at least, have either been watered down from the original adult version or so sanitised that they can seem trivial, light-hearted or childish. Or sometimes they have been reworked so much that only a faint trace of the original story or intended message remains.

Folk tales and myths, like the classics of literature discussed in the previous chapter, are also narrative non-fiction because their characters and stories have become reference points for many things in our modern world. We may describe something as being a 'Herculean task' or be jealous of those who have 'the Midas touch' or suggest that what is needed is a 'round-table discussion', even if we have never read the stories of Heracles (Hercules in the Roman version), King Midas or King Arthur in their original forms. The difference between these traditional stories and the works of literature discussed in the last chapter is that traditional stories usually have no single author and no record of their first oral telling.

In 1999, Ingpen took part in a Victorian Education Department program about visual literacy, in which he held a filmed conversation with two secondary students. He had been chosen because he had just published his companion books, *Fabulous Places of Myth* (1998) and *Once upon a Place* (1999), from which much about visual literacy could be learned. He started by telling the students:

'There are three sorts of stories: real stories, ones where elements of reality have been wrapped in imagination, and completely imagined ones. I am an illustrator — purely and simply. My world leaps between the real and the imagined and I settle somewhere between the two.'

Ingpen introduced the students to the metaphor of the forest of the imagination, discussed in the previous chapter, and its companion metaphor: the 'marginal world' which he describes as 'a place between reality and fantasy where creatures of the imagination roam onto the borders of daily life', a place not unlike 'that inter-tidal zone on the beach between the land and the sea: a fringe where two different worlds overlap'.

The viewer could see puzzled expressions creep across the faces of the two students. Ingpen was testing the water with them, to see how far they would go with him into these metaphors, and when he casually remarked that 'journeys like this take time — you can't get back from Valhalla as quickly as you would like, to answer the phone', the students seemed to be thinking, 'He's an adult. Adults don't usually act like this. He is play-acting, isn't he?' They were, of course, far too polite to ask these questions aloud, and Ingpen's passion for traditional literature was far too convincing — so it wasn't long before they were 'sucked in' and busy discussing his journeys to these places.

First stop on their journey that day was Hamelin Town. As Ingpen's notes indicate (p.48), the town still exists. The pictures he brought back from his journey to Hamelin Town give a better understanding of the folktale. It is often seen as a cautionary tale about the importance of keeping one's word — but the fragment of truth that Ingpen wrapped in his illustrations helped account for the 'apparently illogical' nature of the tale. He chose to illustrate the story as an early example of group grief counselling, and in so doing introduced the historical context of the story to a new generation.

Ingpen is convinced that, although these traditional stories are really well crafted, they have lasted for so long not just because of the satisfying story element, but because they bring universal truths to the reader in any age. Folktales and myths at work are relevant to a better understanding of his narrative non-fiction work — they shine a light on the way his illustrations work. Their real power in the context of traditional literature is that, although he is conserving a path to where the stories lie, deep in the forest of the imagination, it is usually a different path from the one most people know. It is a path that comes at the story or character from a different angle, giving us a new understanding of the fragment of truth at the heart of the story.

They reveal much about Ingpen as a person, when we consider which stories he has chosen to illustrate and what 'fragment of truth' he has chosen to wrap.

'Noah's Ark in the Deluge' (pp. 50-51) and 'The Tower of Babel' (pp. 52-3) are good examples of his different paths to well-known stories. As in the opening quote, 'One person's myth is another's religious belief.' Like many others, Ingpen believes it is important to treat others' beliefs with respect, and that becoming familiar with them is a good way of getting inside another's culture. He has always been very respectful of indigenous cultures and their religions. He shares with Patricia Wrightson the belief that the 'deep magic' — the most sacred ideas — should be left to the initiated, and so when he was illustrating her work he was very careful not to depict the events or characters, but to concentrate instead on the detail of the bush and the rock instead. (Patricia Wrightson won the Hans Christian Andersen Medal in 1996, the same year as Ingpen.)

Sometimes we become blind to our own myths because we are so familiar with them. It is here that an illustrator plays an important part by bringing them back into our consciousness. Ingpen believes that the illustrator needs to step forward at this point and be obtrusive — not necessarily in his/her style of illustration but in the choice of tales to illustrate. He encourages illustrators to venture into the forest of the imagination and bring back 'fragments of truth' left lying in wait there. His pictures of the Tower of Babel are a good example of a typical Ingpen invitation to reconsider an ancient myth.

He suggests that 'we are looking at a world which has lost touch with the facts, we don't quite know what is fact and what is fiction.' This is the fragment of truth he has chosen to wrap in his depiction of the Tower. Although there is always truth at the centre of myths and folktales, there is usually more than one truth. This is probably because we all have our own version of the truth, and each tale can speak to us in different ways. In Ingpen's view, one of the truths at the heart of the Tower of Babel story is the issue of communication and connection with others, and the lack of imaginative space in people's lives today.

The Poppykettle Adventure
Ingpen has always been fascinated by the sea and has always lived close to it. The ocean, in its many moods, is a theme running through much of his work, from 'Atlantis' (pp. 56–9) to some of his factual illustrations, such as 'Cook's *Endeavour* Among Reefs' (p. 78) and 'Magellan's Journey' (p. 79).

The Voyage of the Poppykettle (in its three versions) is strictly speaking the only work of fiction written by Ingpen to be included in this book. It was included because it is a deliberate experiment in creating a folk tale. The background to this story, and briefly, the story itself, are described in the caption on page 60. The 'experiment' to wrap facts in fiction continues even after nearly twenty-five years.

Understanding the science that inspired the original Poppykettle story helps explain the relationship between traditional non-fiction and Ingpen's fiction. All science was once wrapped in fiction, in that in a pre-scientific age all scientific knowledge and theory of the universe was wrapped in story. The story about El Nino which Ingpen and his United Nations FAO team discovered was circulated throughout schools and in the market-place to help fishermen rediscover old truths about sustainability. What he calls 'first-generation scientific rawness', which is often unpalatable or too complex to understand, can often be made more appealing and understandable through visual or written text — this is what he is trying to do in the Poppykettle experiment.

The other fragment of truth at the heart of the Poppykettle stories is the 'plight and saga of boat people' — an extremely relevant issue today.
We still resort to telling stories as a way of ignoring cold, hard facts about human nature or calling up the most noble human characteristics. It is easy to forget that the monsters 'Beowulf' (pp. 46) fought or the trials Momotaro (p. 46) faced were distilled by the storytellers from the things we least understand and most fear about our own natures. By demonising the enemies, the storytellers justified our brutal attacks on them, and by making fun of the enemies, the storytellers reassured us by making them appear less threatening. So the problem for the illustrator here is slightly different to those posed in the previous chapter. Although most of these stories are set in pre-industrial times, and the architecture, costumes and people need to be represented accurately, the prime objective is not historical accuracy but finding the truth at the heart of the story and then carefully wrapping it, so that the next person can unwrap it for themselves.

Storytellers wrapped the truths of myths and folktales in such clever and subtle ways that only long after the chills had subsided or the laughter evaporated were they discovered and acknowledged by the listener. Ingpen's illustrations of folk tales and myths at work reveal what a clever and subtle visual storyteller of his time he is.

CHAPTER THREE

Facts in Focus

It is easy to overlook the process involved in illustrating facts. For those of us who are not illustrators, factual pictures seem straightforward — the illustrator is simply capturing a 'real' person, event or object. Of course, illustrators and the visually literate know that it is not as simple as it looks — that angles of vision and other 'tricks' play important roles in the construction of these pictures.

The Crucifixion

The scene I have invented of the place of Christ's crucifixion takes the viewpoint of a bystander who may not have known the importance of the

Machu Picchu, 1500 AD

I had the good fortune to visit this lost city of the Inca high in the Andes at Easter in 1973. On arrival the city was shrouded in cloud, but shortly after I had begun to wonder if the long trip had been wasted, the clouds rose to reveal this scene.

All I had to do, later in 1989 when I needed to make a recreation of the place, was to build walls and roofs on the abandoned site.

The Great Wall of China

This picture is in my book *Encyclopedia of Mysterious Places* (1990). It attemps to recreate a time 2000 years ago when, as the caption says: 'The wall and its watchtowers followed the succession of hilltops across the northern boundaries of China. Here a skirmish is in progress as nomads try to take part of the wall and reinforcements rush in from the Chinese side.'

The Defenestration

Political gestures often seem trivial, but they can have long-lasting effects. So although a few men were thrown out of castle windows in Prague in 1620 on to soft straw, and survived, the offence to the Emperor they represented was enormous. The incident has, rightly or wrongly, been blamed for the Thirty Years' War in Europe. The building I have drawn in the picture is based on Stokesay Castle, Shropshire, and is often my reference for such buildings in period illustrations of fact and fiction. Somebody once counted that I had used it eight times in different projects.

The Bastille, July 1789

It did not matter that the Bastille in Paris contained only a handful of prisoners when it was stormed in July 1789. With its massive walls and its history as a prison for repressed people, it offered a difficult subject to illustrate. To show the actual storming of the gates from a suitable vantage point, I had to hire a group to demolish the tenement houses surrounding the prison in order to see the point of action. At least that is what it looks like in the picture.

75

Industry and Technology *and* Turnips in Agriculture

To draw upon the style of past illustrators and painters in the same way that we call upon past thinkers and writers is often a powerful way of dating and placing a picture of association. Here are two examples of this play with recognised styles. Bruegel is clearly present in the whimsical 'turnip celebration' that happened in England during this time. And Turner, the great English painter, is the clear influence for the picture telling the story of industrial and technological advances that were happening around him during his life in the late 18th and early 19th centuries, and then on to today.

Industry and Technology

Five things combine here to tell a story. In the composition and atmosphere captured by J. M. Turner in the late 18th century, the light globe, rocket, steam ship and motor car come together.

Turnips in Agriculture

There was such great enthusiasm for the turnip in its role as 'agricultural improver' during the 18th century that its advocates might well have been accused of 'turnip worship'.

76

**Cook's *Endeavour*
among Reefs**
At sunset on 11 June 1770,
Captain James Cook spotted
the first coral shoal he had
ever seen. He sailed carefully
and everything seemed to be
going well, when at 11 p.m.
the *Endeavour* struck the Great
Barrier Reef.

Magellan's Journey
On 28 November 1520, the
small ships of Ferdinand
Magellan crashed out of the
straits that would be called
after him to enter the Pacific
Ocean on their long journey
around the world.

Scott at the South Pole

On 17 January 1912 Captain Scott and his party of four found the Norwegian flag, the tent and food left by Amundsen at the South Pole. He wrote in his diary:
'The South Pole. We've made it… It is a terrible day. We are tired… Great God, what an awful place! To have endured so much and not to be the first, is a terrible disappointment.'

Sled Dog, Penguins and Phonograph

The ill-fated Scott Expedition of 1912 was delayed by bad weather and much time was spent waiting for conditions to improve to make a dash for the South Pole. They listened to records played on phonographs which in those days was 'state of the art in recording'. So I played a visual joke in my reference to 'His Master's Voice' advertising, and introduced a few local penguins.

Model T Ford Production Line, 1913

The automobile was a product ideally suited to mass production, although I was to discover that almost no photos had ever been taken of the process used by Henry Ford in his Detroit factory. After many preliminary drawings this final picture shows the part-finished cars being rolled down an assembly line. Here, completed chassis have been made on the ground level, while bodies and seats have been assembled on the floor above. The bodies could then be lowered on to the chassis and bolted into place to make the finished cars.

Halloween Circus

Over a year or more publisher and designer Michael Neugebauer and I worked on planning, illustrating and publishing a special book to capture the spirit of Halloween, a book with surprises beyond just the words and pictures.

Here are sequences of communications that record the progress of our working together:

28 January, 2000 [Ingpen to Neugebauer]

Halloween Circus — I have given this a good deal of thought, particularly since you have encouraged me to explore 'visual tricks and hidden images'. Today I will post to you a dummy (black and white only) of my present thinking of how the book might work. It is full of surprises, but not entirely visual ones ...'

26 June, 2000 [Neugebauer to Ingpen]

I am very happy and excited about the progress in the Halloween book. We are certainly working in the direction which will make the idea and concept work. It does need more of a continuation when opening it. First endpaper, first foldout, then turn a page or two and fold out the big front endpaper. The following pages must fit into it as you indicated. Then we can ask the reader to start folding out the endpaper on the back. First foldout, then turn a few pages and at the end both endpapers are folded out like a huge poster. All centre pages integrate. We must try to build up more tension ...'

26 September, 2001 [Neugebauer to Ingpen]

Halloween — they all [our foreign co-publishers] just love it and they want to go ahead with the prepress production and possibly publish the book next fall ... I am so excited to get the book started, do the colour separations the day after tomorrow in Italy and possibly have dummies for Frankfurt [Frankfurt Book Fair, October]

26 October, 2001 [Ingpen to Neugebauer]

How did you go at Frankfurt with Halloween?

Facts in Focus

Ingpen's depiction of the crucifixion of Christ (p. 70) is one of the strongest of his factual illustrations. Christ's life and death have inspired, and continue to inspire, countless visual representations. The dilemma facing Ingpen was how to illustrate anew an event that is sacred to many and known by many more. The angle he has chosen for the crucifixion gives the picture its strength. His placement of Christ off to the left (see caption, p. 71) and the way he has positioned the viewer, give the impression that the viewer is an 'uninvited bystander' at an event, the full significance of which will not be recognised until many years later. Ingpen did this to create a feeling of humility in the viewer .

For Ingpen, illustrating facts is all about knowing when to use various approaches to 'lift the emotional level' so that his pictures do more than just 'communicate an event, person or scene'. There are times when tricks are needed and others, such as Machu Picchu (p. 72), when they are not. Following the lead of N.C.Wyeth, Ingpen is a great believer in the obvious but often over-looked practice of finding inspiration and the solution to an illustrative problem by actually going to the place. The picture of Machu Picchu is a good example of the mystery of a place working its own magic. Ingpen did not need to 'tweak' his picture to make it more interesting. As he says, the place and all it represents 'is so steeped in mystery' that nothing else is needed.

'Tweaking' was needed for his pictures of 'The Defenestration' (p. 74) and 'The Bastille' (p. 75), since Ingpen was at neither event, and needed to capture the fact at the heart of these political stories. He used humour in 'The Defenestration' to show how an event can blow out of all proportion to its original intent. In 'The Bastille' he chose to depict the issue of access — for the republicans there at the time — and for himself as an illustrator centuries later. To do this, as the caption relates, he had to organise for some deconstruction of the surrounding buildings to occur so that he could paint at a safe, but close, vantage point. The way this painting is constructed gives us visual access to an historic building, echoing the symbolism of the storming of the Bastille.

As a conserver of historical ideas, Ingpen needs to find ways to help today's readers grasp the full significance of certain moments and movements in history. One of the things he is trying to do is 'loosen up the mind of the reader' so that he or she is more interested. He grabs our attention in

'Turnips in Agriculture' (p. 77) and makes us wonder, 'Why does a turnip have such a prominent position?' We may laugh at the importance of the humble turnip to agricultural practices in the 18th Century, but Ingpen's whimsical painting helps us to understand it. His visual reference to Bruegel, observing ordinary people going about their daily life, captures a feeling of the time. He has used a similar technique in 'Industry and Technology' (p. 76), by referring to the work of J.M.Turner to capture the atmosphere of change at the time of the industrial revolution — a time when the speed of development changed into a higher gear. This visual reference also contains a note of warning about the pollution that will ensue.

Creating a sense of danger is one of the most evocative tools an illustrator can use — but the illustrator has to know how and when to use it to best effect. For instance, it is important that a painting does not 'run aground' on stereotypical ways of calling up danger. 'Cook's *Endeavour* among Reefs' (p.78) is a perfect example of a painting where 'nothing seems to be happening', even though history tells us that a momentous event is about to occur. Ingpen could have overdramatised the situation — what was his reason for not doing so? He used Cook's log entries as research for this picture and found no trace of dramatics there, even though it was such an awful moment for Cook as a captain. This visual understatement leaves space for the viewer; the picture sets the scene for the situation to take place. This is a risk for the illustrator — the viewer may not take up the offer of space and so overlook the picture altogether. Perhaps this is why visual stereotypes are used so often — they are easier for the illustrator to use and the viewer to understand.

In contrast, Ingpen's picture of 'Scott at the South Pole' (pp. 80–81) is an example of an illustrator underplaying a feeling of desperate disappointment to reinforce the tragedy of Scott's expedition. He uses a ragged old tent that has half blown away to underscore the despair Scott's party must have felt on reaching the South Pole, only to discover they had been beaten there by Amundsen's party. The tragedy is compounded because we know that all Scott's party died on the way home.

There are, however, times when dramatics and a heightened sense of the theatrical must be used, and *Halloween Circus* (pp. 84–5) is a wonderful example of the book as theatre.

Gandhi of India

During his legendary 'Salt March' in 1930 Gandhi made this plea to anybody who would listen:

'I want world sympathy in this battle of right against might.'

CHAPTER FOUR   **Joining up the Dots**

For most of us the earliest memories of the excitement of making a picture came when we were introduced to the magic of 'dot-to-dot' puzzles. As young children we were presented with a page of black dots, all numbered, and our challenge was to join them together with a pencil and discover that they made a picture of something we recognised. The result gave us joy, both in discovering and revealing something from nothing, and in being able to do that all by ourselves, and then in going on to colour it in and complete 'our' picture.

The big difference between us now as adult, trained illustrators, and when we were children, is that our job, our intellectual and imaginative responsibility, is to invent or find the dots. Having done this we must put them on paper so that when we join them we have the foundation of a picture. Our sketch books and note pads are full of evidence of our search for dots, and positions for them in relation to each other. The dots we seek are those that display the substance of the story our picture is to tell, not just the outline of form.

In some cases the dots we find in preparation for a picture actually fall out and disappear, leaving an 'unfinished space'. This is what I call imaginative space — a place for the viewer to dwell, to collect their thoughts, to add their own shapes and interpretations to the picture.

Robert Ingpen, 2002

Hands of the Poor

There is much for the viewer
to think about in the spaces
left here between the drawing
of hands and arms and the
words of Mother Theresa.

'You must know the poor
In order to love them.
You must love the poor
In order to serve them!'

Chief Seattle

In 1854 Isaac Stevens, the new Governor of Indian Affairs for the Washington Territories, visited the Indian tribes in Puget Sound, told them that the government planned to buy their land and pressed them to move to reservations. Chief Seattle, the Indian tribal leader, is reported to have reacted with these words: 'As their message left the mouth of the translator I saw anger burn in the eyes of our young people. But as an old man I listened more in sorrow than in anger. Anger and hatred only bring pain ... We could not hope to defeat them. When their leaders pressed us for an answer I rose to my feet slowly and pointed at the sky and began my reply.'

The reply by Chief Seattle that day was recorded by Dr Henry Smith, who later published his version in the Seattle *Sunday Star*. This is the earliest and most accurate version of the Chief's famous speech and plea for nature. Through his speech he lives on as an inspiration and guide to living in harmony with the earth. As he said, 'My words are like stars. They do not set.'

How can one sell the air?
How can one own the earth?
Every shining pine needle, every sighing shore,
Every grassy clearing, every humming insect,
Are holy in the memory and experience
Of my people.

Have you heard the music of flowing waters?
The rivers are sacred to us.
Each ghostly reflection in the clear water
Of the lakes tells of events and memories
In the life of my people.
The water's gurgle is the voice of my father's father.
The rivers are our brothers; they quench our thirst.
Between the tender arms of their banks,
They carry our canoes where they will.

Have you felt the wind darting over
The surface of the pond?
Have you smelt the breeze cleansed by a midday shower
The air is precious to the red man,
For all things share it, the beasts, the trees, and man.
It is here with us from first to last,
It gives us our breath and receives our last sigh.

Have you stroked the trunk of a tree, a blade of grass?
Have you felt the sap which courses through them?
We are part of the earth and it is part of us.
The earth is our mother.
The perfumed flowers are our sisters.

93

The bear, the great condor, are our brothers,
The rocky crests, the meadows, the ponies and man
All belong to our family.
Now the white men have come.
Our ways are different from your ways,
And we do not understand what living becomes
When all the buffalo are slaughtered,
The wild horses tamed, the forests plundered.
Where is the thicket? Gone.
Where is the eagle? Gone.
What is there to living if a man cannot hear the cry
Of the thrush or the arguments of the frogs
94   Around the pond at night?

What is it the whiteman wishes to buy?
My people ask me.
The idea is strange to us.
How can you buy or sell the sky?
The warmth of the land, the swiftness of the deer?
These things do not belong to us.
How can we sell them to you? How can you buy them?
Is the earth yours to do what you want with
Just because we sign a piece of paper?
Can you buy back the buffalo once the last one has died?

The Melbourne Cricket Ground History Tapestry

To mark 150 years of the Melbourne Cricket Ground (1853–2003), I was commissioned to tell the story of heroic achievements and magnificent occasions on the 'Paddock' over that time. The tapestry was woven in wool, 7 metres long and 2 metres high. The weaving took seven months and was done by the skilled craft weavers of the Victorian Tapestry Workshop, Melbourne. The completed tapestry will hang on public view

in the new buildings under construction to replace and modernise the old stands surrounding the northern boundary of the famous ground.

In the tapestry over two hundred figures were chosen to take their place in the picture story. People who have figured in the development and progress of the games of cricket and Australian Rules Football; events like the Olympic Games of 1956; Austral Wheel Racing and concerts by international performers. Each figure is only about 22cm tall, so there was no chance to achieve details in the weave of facial features. The identification of each individual relies upon the action they are remembered for, and the costume they wore to represent their country in cricket, or club in football.

Robert Ingpen sits down to work. His studio faces east and overlooks an Australian garden. When asked about the difference between a painter and an illustrator he often observes that a painter stands to work and an illustrator always sits.

A view from the garden of Angela and Robert's home at Anglesea near the Great Ocean Road, Victoria, Australia

Joining up the dots

'Joining up the dots' is a metaphor that Ingpen uses to explain the art of illustration. The metaphor works on many levels — from individual pictures through to the decisions an illustrator makes about his or her own body of work. Unlike for 'join-the-dot' pictures from childhood, the illustrator not only has to find the dots, but also decide which ones to leave out.
Ingpen's lifelong commitment to the art of the book is clearly evident in his design for *Halloween Circus* (p. 85). The book is a good example of the difference he sees between studying fine art and studying illustration:

'As a tertiary study, fine art teaches theory and the processes of art which stands alone; that is art which does not require binding or reproduction and which is not created to work in conjunction with text.'

The production values of *Halloween Circus,* and the engineering involved in the 'Ingpen fold', have upped the ante for publishers and illustrators alike. As he writes in the caption, it is a design Ingpen thought would not come into existence. The fold opens in such a way as to create a backdrop like no other. It comes alive as an active participant in the story. The characters and events of *Halloween Circus* sweep magically in, out of and across the backdrop and our consciousness. When the reader reaches the end of the story, refolds the backdrop and closes the book, all the fantastic elements are held fast within — in much the same way as the rest of the year holds fast the spirits and possibilities which can only cross over into our world on 31 October each year.

Ingpen continues to be connected to some of the world's most profound movements and people — in Australia, the conservation movement and the establishment of the Dromkeen Children's Literature Centre in Riddells Creek; and internationally in Jane Goodall's Roots and Shoots Foundation, the Eric Carle Museum of Picture Book Art, IBBY and the Bologna Children's Book Fair. He feels that it is important for illustrators to be connected to the book world for purposes of professional renewal and learning, as well as to give something back. Finding ideas and people with whom to connect, and innovative ways of doing this, is another layer of his 'joining-up-the-dots' metaphor. It is about seeking out which projects to pursue, and how best to pursue them — and considering what to illustrate and with whom.
In 1998 Grimm Press commissioned Ingpen to design and illustrate their Great Names Series, illustrated biographies of people who have had a lasting impact on the world. The series includes figures such as Captain Scott, James Cook, Mahatma Gandhi, Mother Theresa and Chief Seattle. This is

the series of books of which Robert is proudest. He describes them as the most simply and effectively presented books he has ever illustrated. The illustrative space he has left and the simplicity with which he has illustrated and designed these books are evidence of his respect, not only for the great names but for Grimm Press in publishing this important series. In making these books, Ingpen says he has gone into the 'territory of the soul and the spirit'. Because the lives of their subjects have had such a profound impact on the world he had to 'dig deeper so that he could make more profound and lasting pictures'.

When Ingpen was urged to add more text to his captions for 'Hands of the Poor' (pp. 90–91) and to the sequence of pictures from Chief Seattle's speech (pp. 93–7), he was emphatic that we had to practise what we have been preaching in *Pictures Telling Stories* and leave readers the space to consider the illustrations from this series for themselves. In the case of the illustrations from Chief Seattle's speech, he designed the sequence to be a 'type of poetry where too many words would interfere with getting your thoughts straight'.

One of the layers of the 'joining-up-the-dots' metaphor concerns knowing when to include dots that may be lying out past the boundaries of book illustration. Ingpen has done this, for example, through sculpture: the Poppykettle, the Dromkeen key and the bronze doors to the Melbourne Cricket Club; through postage stamp and flag design; and through murals and consultancy.

Having accepted a commission to design a tapestry to commemorate the centenary of the Melbourne Cricket Ground, Ingpen's challenge was to decide which figures and events would best represent the history of this famous ground. He then had to decide how best to capture those figures so that people could recognise them, without having the luxury of facial detail to indicate identity. Australia is a sports-mad nation — many Australians joke about the religious status granted to sport — so the question of whom to include and whom to omit was a delicate one.

The theme of conservation is again taken up with Robert's illustrations for *The Drover's Boy*. It may seem strange, but most Australians would know more about the history of the Melbourne Cricket Ground than they would about the practice of cattle drovers taking indigenous companions. Ted Egan's moving song brought this untold Australian story to many. In illustrating the song, Ingpen has created a stunning book which engages readers powerfully, makes a strong statement about the importance of conserving previously untold or hidden stories and takes this story to a wider audience.

Although he prefers to conserve old stories, myths and folktales from the forest of the imagination, there are times when Ingpen uses his illustrative skills to introduce new stories which he believes should be told. It is no secret that Nathaniel Lachenmeyer used the story of a sparrow waking one morning to find his beak broken as a metaphor for mental illness, and the role mental illness plays in forcing people to the margins of life and in some cases, off the page altogether. The story reminds us that we are often too busy to notice the broken people among us. It is easier to ignore the 'other' whose circumstances or actions may cause us distress, or to be angry or judgemental when we see people whose behaviour or appearance puzzles or disgusts us — we can safely hide behind this puzzlement or disgust. It is harder to ignore the reality of the outsider when the facts of the story come wrapped not only in beautiful prose but also in moving and understated illustrations. Ingpen first had to go searching for the dots needed to tell this story; he then had to choose which dots to leave out. The result is enough space for the simple yet wrenching story to work its magic on our sense of compassion and understanding.

A willingness to voice alternative conceptions — to seek out and include less commonly used dots — is something that has underpinned Ingpen's career in illustration. It has seen him swim against the tide by not making a name for himself as an interpretive illustrator, and it is something that he encourages other illustrators to consider:

'Pictures Telling Stories [was written] to help remind people that there is a mainstream [of art and literature] which has come down from the past and it's good for us to be respectful of all this ... we need more than just glib terms such as narrative non-fiction ... it has to do with bridging the gap between fiction and non-fiction — about how the world works ... it's essentially an illustrator who will make the most successful bridge, because [he or she is] making [illustrations] work towards helping others understand.' Ingpen describes his work as 80 per cent intellectual — that is, conceptualising the project. The other 20 per cent, which is the technical side of illustration, he calls the 'tortured colouring in'. He 'colours in' using watercolour — but what sets his dry-brush watercolour apart from many other illustrators' is this rehearsal and planning stage. The actual drawing and painting takes so little of the time because he has spent so long on the intellectual

In 2002 I completed the illustrations for a children's story by Nathaniel Lachenmeyer. *Broken Beaks* is a beautiful story about the friendship between a small sparrow and a homeless man. This powerful narrative, which highlights the heroism and dignity of people with schizophrenia, reaches an important moment when the following text combines with the illustration shown here:

'The stranger looked down and saw a sad, hungry little bird with a broken beak, looking up at him hopefully. 'We're a pair,' he said with a smile. He broke the bread into two equal pieces and gave one to the bird. After eating half in one bite, the stranger stood over the bird to make sure that none of the other birds tried to steal his crumbs.'

issues. He feels that, sadly, these intellectual approaches are not taught to illustrators anymore.

Prospective illustrators would do well to take notice of the formula that has served Ingpen so well for so long. And as viewers of his work we would be well served by spending 80 per cent of our time considering and questioning the intellectual issues he broaches, before spending 20 per cent of our time judging his 'colouring in'!

In 1980 a book entitled *Robert Ingpen* was published in Australia by Macmillan. This was before the pictures that appear in this book had been created, yet the comments made by Michael Page in his conclusion for that earlier book continue to have relevance:

'Robert Ingpen is one of those rare figures on the modern artistic scene: a man with complete control of pure line and pure colour. He desires only to learn how to use them better, without diverting into impressionism or any other technique which may camouflage an artist's true ability. If he belongs to any school, which he would mockingly deny, it is that of representational art.

'The word "representational", invented to describe precise representations of actual objects and scenes, is used deprecatingly by aficionados of modern art. Among artists, the deprecation sometimes increases in proportion to the user's deficiencies in technique. The implication is that an ability to draw and paint accurately is somehow unworthy of true "artists".

'Ingpen himself avoids this kind of discussion or controversy. It is quite difficult to draw him into conversation about art and the subject seems to embarrass him. He sums up his feelings by saying, "I feel sympathy for non-achievers who can't develop a style of their own, and dislike fast-food artists who paint to make money or a name."

'Most discussions of an artist's work tend to seek derivations: the way he or she has been influenced by predecessors. When looking for such derivations in Ingpen's work, one concludes that he continues, in his own style, an ancient and honourable line. It is that of the classicism which developed in Greece and Rome, flourished there unaffected by the surrealism of the orient and radiated in a great elipse through Renaissance Europe into England, and eventually to the Americas and other European colonies.

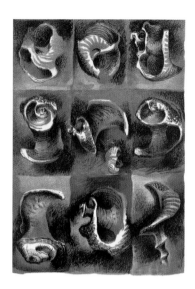

'The Marginal World'
lithographic print, 1958

'It is a style of disciplined creation and confident craftsmanship: a heritage that never has been diverted by theories and arguments. It is indestructible because its absolute certainty cannot be deflected, even though it may be adapted or improved. The purity of a talent always remains inviolate, unless its possessor allows himself to be seduced by fashions.

'This is hardly likely to happen to Ingpen because he does not mingle in the world where artistic fashions are born: that of art reviewers, artist's agents, the patrons of modern art and their entourage.

'Robert Ingpen is completely his own man and he and his work are fully integrated. The integrity of his art is seen instantly in its strength and precision: the presentation of his subjects in almost tangible modelling, clear line and clear colour, and compositions which by their essential rightness attract and hold the gaze and seem continually to offer a little more. There are no alibis in Robert Ingpen's work.

'His antipathy to "artiness" is reflected in his refusal to call himself an artist. He prefers the term "illustrator", which is an impossibly modest description. However this self-separation from the world of art does not imply a feeling of superiority. He sets himself such high standards that he is embarrassed by the possibility of having to give an opinion on the work of someone whose standards are not equally high.

'Once I remarked to him that many people might think him very unlike the conventional picture of an artist. Superficially his life is that of any middle-class family man who has done rather well at his chosen profession, whereas the traditional idea of an artist is that he or she should be a rebel against conformity. He said, "But I am a rebel. A rebel against mediocrity".'

Peter Pan drawings, c.1943

Chronology

1936	Born 13 October, East Melbourne. Lived in Geelong, Victoria, Australia
1942–1954	Educated at the Geelong College
1955–8	Studied Art and Design at the Royal Melbourne Institute of Technology Graduated with Diploma specialising in 'Art of the Book'
1958	Employed as Communication Designer with the CSIRO (Commonwealth Scientific and Industrial Research Organisation)
1963	Designed and painted THE LAND RESEARCH MURAL, CSIRO Division of Land Research, Black Mountain, Canberra
1966	Published 'The Representation of Relations in Biotic Systems', Kesteven and Ingpen, *Proceedings of the Ecological Society of Australia*, vol. 1, 79-83
1968	Designed and painted THE CLUNIES ROSS MEMORIAL MURAL, Clunies Ross House, Carlton, Melbourne Resigned from CSIRO and began freelance design and illustration in Melbourne
1969	Developmental consultant to the Swan Hill Pioneer Settlement Designed and painted the GEELONG CITY HALL MURAL Designed postage stamps for Australia Post
1970	Designed and painted THE CONSERVATION MURAL, Arthur Rylah Enviromental Instute, Melbourne Designed COOK BICENTENARY STAMP series
1971	Appointed Expert Consultant to FAO/UNDP Program on Fisheries, Mexico. Report published 'Information Function in Fisheries', FAO
1972	Designed PIONEER LIFE STAMP series for Australia Post Wrote and illustrated PIONEER SETTLEMENT IN AUSTRALIA and PIONEERS OF WOOL (Rigby)
1973	Appointed Expert Consultant to FAO/UNDP Program on Fisheries, IMARPE, Peru. Report published: *Models and Reality — The Anchovy*
1974	Illustrated STORM BOY by Colin Thiele (Rigby)
1975	Designed and illustrated WESTERNPORTRAIT (Victorian Conservation). Wrote and illustrated ROBE — A PORTRAIT OF THE PAST (Rigby)
1976	Designed and illustrated THE RUNAWAY PUNT, text by Michael Page (Rigby) Designed and illustrated MELBOURNE ZOO literature and enclosures Designed and painted the GEELONG WOOL HISTORY MURAL, CBA Bank Member of the Interim Planning Council for Deakin University Member of Council, The Geelong College Designed and illustrated SURPRISE AND ENTERPRISE, text by McKay (CSIRO)
1977	Designed and painted the GEELONG WATER MURAL, Geelong Water Trust. Illustrations completed for COMMERCIAL FISH OF AUSTRALIA (Department of Primary Industry, Canberra)
1978	Designed and illustrated PARADISE AND BEYOND (Tasmania) by Nick Evers (Rigby) Designed and illustrated LINCOLN'S PLACE by Colin Thiele (Rigby)

El Nino and his Pelican Slaves

A detail from the cover artwork for a scientific report written in Peru in 1973. The report is entit-led 'Models and Reality — Research into the Anchovy'.

IBBY Poster for Hans Christian Andersen birthday, April 1988

1978	Commissioned to design Insignia for The Northern Territory, Australia Concept design for The Werribee Zoological Park (Melbourne Zoo)
1979	Wrote and illustrated AUSTRALIAN GNOMES (Rigby) Wrote and illustrated MARKING TIME — AUSTRALIA'S ABANDONED BUILDINGS (Rigby) Illustrated RIVER MURRAY MARY by Colin Thiele (Rigby)
1980	Designed and illustrated TURNING POINTS IN THE MAKING OF AUSTRALIANS, text by Michael Page (Rigby) Book published by Macmillan, ROBERT INGPEN — compiled by Angela Ingpen with text by Michael Page Consultant to The Great Barrier Reef Marine Park Authority. Report 'On Behalf of the Reef' and applications for World Heritage inclusion Wrote and illustrated THE VOYAGE OF THE POPPYKETTLE (Rigby) Designed THE POPPYKETTLE FOUNTAIN, Geelong Waterfront
1981	Wrote and illustrated AUSTRALIA'S HERITAGE WATCH (Rigby) Wrote and illustrated THE UNCHOSEN LAND (Rigby) Illustrated NIGHT OF THE MUTTONBIRDS by Mary Small (Methuen)
1982	Designed and illustrated AUSSIE BATTLERS, text by Michael Page (Rigby) Illustrated CLANCY OF THE OVERFLOW by A. B. Paterson (Rigby)
1983	Illustrated LIFETIMES by B. Melonie (Hill of Content)
1984	Illustrated CLICK GO THE SHEARS (Rigby) Designed CONSERVATION POSTERS, South Australian Government Designed and illustrated THE GREAT BULLOCKY RACE, text by Michael Page (Hill of Content)
1985	Illustrated RELIGIOUS WORLDS by Max Charlesworth (Hill of Content) Illustrated COLONIAL SOUTH AUSTRALIA, text by Michael Page (J.M.Dent) Designed and painted JUPITERS MURAL, Broadbeach Casino, Queensland
1986	Wrote and illustrated THE IDLE BEAR (Lothian) Designed and illustrated THE ENCYCLOPAEDIA OF THINGS THAT NEVER WERE, text by Michael Page (Rigby) Awarded The Hans Christian Andersen Medal for Children's Literature (illustration)
1987	Designed and illustrated CONSERVATION by Margaret Dunkle (Hill of Content) Designed and illustrated FOLKTALES AND FABLES OF THE WORLD by B. Hayes (Bateman) Designed and illustrated THE MAKING OF AUSTRALIANS, text by Michael Page (Dent)

1988	Illustrated THE NARGAN AND THE STARS by Patricia Wrightson (Hutchinson)

1988   Illustrated THE NARGAN AND THE STARS by Patricia Wrightson (Hutchinson)
Designed and illustrated series of short tales by Charles Dickens and Mark Twain (Scholastic)
Design of BRONZE DOORS, Entrance to Melbourne Cricket Club
Exhibition at the Geelong Art Gallery, THE ART OF ROBERT INGPEN (Oct.-Jan. 1988)
Wrote and illustrated THE AGE OF ACORNS (Lothian)

1989   Illustrated THE GREAT DEEDS OF SUPERHEROES by Maurice Saxby (Millenium)
Awarded The Dromkeen Medal

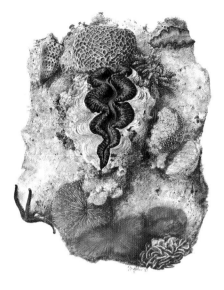

1990   Illustrated THE GREAT DEEDS OF HEROIC WOMEN by Maurice Saxby (Millenium)
Designed and illustrated ENCYCLOPAEDIA OF MYSTRIOUS PLACES, text by P. Wilkinson (Dragon's World)

1991   Designed and illustrated ENCYCLOPAEDIA OF WORLD EVENTS, text by P.Wilkinson(Dragon's World)

1992   Illustrated TREASURE ISLAND by R. L. Stevenson (Dragon's World)

1993   Designed and illustrated ENCYCLOPAEDIA OF IDEAS THAT CHANGED THE WORLD, text by P. Wilkinson (Dragon's World)

1994   Designed and illustrated A CELEBRATION OF CUSTOMS AND RITUALS, text by P. Wilkinson (Dragon's World)

1994   Wrote and illustrated THE DREAMKEEPER (Lothian)

1996   Built a new home at Anglesea

1997   Designed and illustrated THE DROVER'S BOY by Ted Egan (Lothian)
Wrote and illustrated THE AFTERNOON TREEHOUSE (Lothian)
Designed and illustrated THE BOY FROM NURNBURG, text by Ejnar Agertoft (Agertoft)

1998   Designed and illustrated FABULOUS PLACES OF MYTH, text by Michael Cave (Lothian)
International exhibition in Taipei, Taiwan.
Designed and illustrated books for Grimm Press, Taiwan (CAPTAIN SCOTT, JAMES COOK,
MARCO POLO, and XUAN ZANG in the Great Names series.)

1999   Illustrated AROUND THE WORLD IN EIGHTY DAYS by Jules Verne (Arena)
Wrote and illustrated ONCE UPON A PLACE (Lothian)
Retold and illustrated THE POPPYKETTLE PAPERS (Pavilion)

2000   Designed and illustrated for Grimm Press GANDHI, MOTHER THERESA, and CHIEF SEATTLE
Designed and illustrated H. C. ANDERSEN, text by Sorenson (Agertoft)
Wrote and illustrated A BEAR TALE (Lothian)
Designed and illustrated WHO IS THE WORLD FOR?, text by T. Pow (Walker)

2001   Designed and illustrated SHAKESPEARE — HIS WORK AND HIS WORLD by Michael Rosen (Walker)
Designed and illustrated ROBINSON CRUSOE by Daniel Defoe (Grimm Press)

2002   Designed THE MELBOURNE CRICKET GROUND TAPESTRY and 200 detail drawings for weaving during 2002-3 by the Victorian Tapestry Workshop
Designed and illustrated PINOCCHIO by Carlo Collodi (Grimm Press)
Designed and illustrated HALLOWEEN CIRCUS, text by C. Neugebauer (Neugebauer)
Designed and illustrated THE MAGIC CRYSTAL, text by B. Weninger (Neugebauer)
Illustrations for A WIZARD'S BOOK OF SPELLS (Palazzo)

2003   Designed and illustrated BROKEN BEAKS by Nathaniel Lachenmeyer (Michelle Anderson)

Coral Rock Community (upside and underside), drawn at Heron Island, Great Barrier Reef, 1980

Catalogue of Reproduced Illustrations

Robert Ingpen's art that appears in this book has been created to be published in books over the past twenty years or so.

For more information about his work there are a number of websites. These include the National Library of Australia Archive.

For information about current exhibitions, continuing exhibitions, and original artwork viewing and sale, contact should be made with Sadrene Smith, Melaleuca Gallery of Fine Art, Anglesea, Australia 3230.
Email:
s1smith@melaleuca.com.au
www.melaleuca.com.au

Sarah Mayor Cox

Sarah Mayor Cox worked as a primary teacher and teacher-librarian in Melbourne before taking up her current position as a lecturer in English Education at La Trobe University, Bendigo, Australia.

She is a founding and current member of the Children's Book Council of Australia (CBCA), Bendigo Sub-Branch; a member of the Victorian Executive of the CBCA; a founding and current convenor of the Biennial La Trobe University, Bendigo, Children's Literature Conferences; and a former President of the Central Victorian Local Council of the Australian Literacy Educators Association.

Sarah is a co-author of *Success with Reading and Writing: Helping At-risk Students 8–13 years*, Teacher Manual and Student Log (Rowe, Lamont, Daly, Edwards and Cox, Dellasta, Melbourne, 2000).

In her spare time she reviews and writes articles on children's and Young Adult books and she is currently working on a biography of Robert Ingpen's work for her Ph.D.

Sarah would like to thank Heather and Harold Chatfield for being so interested in this project and Pete and the boys — Oliver, Hamish and Samuel — for their patience when she couldn't come out to play.

A Midsummer Night's Dream
(*Endpapers*)
In the comedy A Midsummer Night's Dream, Shakespeare moves very quickly between three groups of characters: lords and ladies; workmen; and fairies. What looks like a bit of supernatural fun turns out to be much more.